Labor Day at Venice Beach

Labor Day at Venice Beach

Poems by J.D. Smith

Cherry Grove Collections

Published by Cherry Grove Collections
P.O. Box 541106
Cincinnati, OH 45254-1106

ISBN: 9781936370870
LCCN: 2012945223

Poetry Editor: Kevin Walzer
Business Editor: Lori Jareo

Visit us on the web at www.cherry-grove.com

Acknowledgments

Acknowledgment is gratefully made to the following publications in which some of this collection's poems appeared, sometimes in different form:

32 Poems, Alimentum, Arabesques, Arkansas Review, Babel, Big Happy, Erete, Gargoyle, The Helix Magazine, Hiss Quarterly, Innisfree Poetry, Junctures, Leafpond, Lilliput Review, Los Angeles Review, New Press, Out of Line, The Pedestal Magazine, 99 Poems for the 99 Percent, Poems Niederngasse, Punchnel's, Shape of a Box, South American Explorer, Terrain, Umbrella and Verse Wisconsin.

"Questions on Recruitment" appeared in the anthology *Against Agamemnon* (Water Wood Press).

Further acknowledgment is very gratefully made to the National Endowment for the Arts, the Anam Cara Retreat Center, and the Virginia Center for the Creative Arts for financial support and for time, studio space and encouragement in the preparation of this collection.

In memory of my mother, Sandra Lee Smith

Table of Contents

4

1

First Memory

Wisconsin Dells

The kind of Plains Indians
once played by Italians
danced around a fire
that brought to light
feather-swaying headdresses
and the weaving paths
of moccasins made from buckskin
or what passed for it.

The chanting ended with what
white ears heard as "hey-a-ho,"
and the hired tribe took its bows.
The audience rose.
Among them I was carried
into years that would not hold
summer camp or Europe,
or anyone who could tell of them.
Those who had brought me here
could afford this much.
They spent it, and more,
according to my need.

In a used Oldsmobile
I fell asleep on a ride
over gravel roads
that were, if dark,
straight and real.

Transport

The closest I've come to transcendence
was one morning on the train
to Chicago and an internship
that went nowhere,
as many do.

A column without substance, or beyond it,
encompassed me and—
I knew, as well, without proof—
greater heights and depths.
The column turned, switched tracks,
embraced rickety lengths of rail.
Within it *Wall Street Journals*,
now fan corals in a womb-warm reef,
waved to anyone who watched.
Watching, I was myself
and a bright fish in this water,
which was something else
that flowed from a silence
admitting of no name.

I might have pointed, if I could have
pointed in all directions at once
and back to the inside of my fingertips,
as if this essence needed my pointing.

The given morning spread before me
in all its fullness.
I scraped gum off my left loafer,
and I went to work.

Aged Parents

After William Meredith

Who *are* these grizzled children
with the same names as Mom and Dad,
sometimes wearing the same fraying clothes
they would not replace while saving
for our braces, our schooling?

Suddenly—since last week,
or twenty years ago—
they are drawn like pouches
of something, such as vigor,
nearly emptied.

After decades of our *why* and *why not*,
Where is or *What happens when?*
it is their turn to ask questions:
Can you reach this shelf for me?
Would you help me up the stairs?
Their queries may extend to
What is your name?
as if they had not, day after day,
spoken us into being.
We may answer, but on no good authority,
knowing what is now beyond our reach.

Bereaved

The first Christmas *after*—
an orange bristling with cloves,
the mandrill faces
in walnut halves left untouched—
the background, snowbanks
blank as absence.

Metaphors of a Mother's Death

The State

Here is the far country, the distant shore,
before us, the fabled, dreaded land,
the third pole left out of
navigators' maps
and implicit in them.
At the border stands a cart
with drips and monitors powered down,
a fringe of useless tubes.
Its capital: a hollow
in still-warm sheets.

A Game

Red Rover, Red Rover, let Sandra *come over!*
She runs at, and does not break, the line,
and is added to the distant, invisible team.
When my name is called,
will she join in the chant,
stand fast as I cross the field?

Tableau Vivant

An open-beaked fledgling
looks to be fed and, hopping,
chases the air.

Mansion

One can pace the wide halls for hours
without stepping on the same tile twice.
Vacancy is the motif.
Replacing the sky are a ceiling's vaults
illuminated by a single constellation.
There is one door, bolted from outside,
and within are many rooms and great spaces,
the rest of a life to learn them.

Fifteen *Jisei*

1.
Let's see
if the burning
outlasts the candle.

2.
By an invisible rope
I am hanged
from the clouds.

3.
Egg, tadpole, frog—
then what the frog becomes.

4.
A melon left on the vine
until the flesh
outgrows its skin.

5.
A robe
laid out at my birth
now fits.

6.
To be released
from four seasons,
or bound to a fifth.

7.
A petal falls
on breaking ice
and floats downstream.

8.
This reflection
will weigh down
no more puddles.

9.
Moss that grew ten thousand years
would not offer shade, or bear a plum.

10.
One last oar-stroke
between a shore I've forgotten
and one I've never seen.

11.
In bottomless water
a salmon's leap
begins and ends.

12.
Ice water
cools the cup,
then the encircling hand.

13.
Noon sun, full moon—
two more coins
that buy me nothing now.

14.
There is air,
there is water,
and no bubble.

15.
Time to pay for the bowl
that has kept the rice
from spilling, losing flavor.

Day of My Death

A bright watch nestles in my pocket,
loose change swells in a jar,
to pawn, to hoard against the last rainy day
when I am supposed to be broke forever
but will lie, instead, with women
who once stood aloof.

More will follow after I claim my birthright
of a deep, broad cloak, a rounded roof
that no wind will prevail against.

I could lay hold of them tonight.

Still, as a bather is breeze-cooled
before he joins a wave,
to be near is, for now, enough.

I wait, as on a night
of reading in bed until I yawn,
eyes watering, seeing double.
Only then will I take in sleep
like a rich, well-earned drink.

Autumnal

A sky of the same blue as Paul Newman's eyes
presides over one of the last leafy afternoons
before the branches empty, marking
another stretch of joblessness and debt
toward the death that Aurelius said
should interrogate each moment
with the question *Is this*
the thing whose passing I fear?

This, like car wrecks and toothaches,
heartbreaks that won't repeat themselves,
like high school and the suspect nostalgia for it?

The passing to regret:
this hour's maple-red, oak brown.

2

Nocturne

It is too dark to tell
a white thread from a black,
a man's silhouette from a woman's.

A finger and what it meets—
wall or air—
are a continuum.

The line between near and far
is subsumed in this dark,

unbroken by thunder, undone
by gunshot no more
than a fist disperses fog.

It admits no answer
but a low voice
full and round as itself,
fitting like a hand
over another's hand,

a model of forgiveness
or its simulacrum.

Coyotes

Having lingered in green margins and outskirts,
they enter the cities from which we sprawl
as if searching for a prodigal son.

Like the tricksters they are in legend,
one makes us wonder how
a German shepherd got so thin;
another, if a wolf has escaped from the zoo.

At close range,
they resemble only themselves,
defined by great ears and bottlebrush tails,
padding across lawns on their way
to leavings that would otherwise fatten
the raccoon and opossum
once taken by cougar and bear.

Spotted in a floodlight, they gaze back
as if about to pose a question.

Their howling as they bear away
untended dogs, and those dogs' howling,
bespeaks in tooth and claw a rebuke
for acts we are still learning to name.

Elegy

Dusk. The plangent geese migrate.
Ragged chevrons that used to bisect a continent
now settle near a golf course and the retaining pond
of an office park, small oxymoron
inside the larger, land development.
The flocks will rest in head-tucked clusters,
low, transient monoliths, like modest gods
left by a miniature people.

Still, the land-crossing cry
persists as if to close
not a day, but a season,
and mark its loss
with a portion of the brokenness
that informs the haiku's heart
and the weightless bone, somewhere in my heart,
that is struck and softened
by the sentimental string arrangement
that bathes the climax
of a made-for-TV film
about the latest disease
or another private distress
raised to a social issue, if not elevated:
all is forgiven, by everyone, at death's door.
Inevitably as that death,
the notes well up, break forth,
and with them my tears.

¡Pendejo que soy!
The small tide breaks
against my reason.
¡Pendejo que soy!

Literally, in Spanish,
what a pubic hair, meaning fool, I am.
Even my confession is reduced.
In Latin Augustine cried *Mea saura!*
Literally, what a lizard I am,
meaning the serpent's cousin,
and hardly less intimate
with the foot-hardened ground.
Mea maxima saura!
What a great lizard I am,
shouted across the gulf
between perdition and salvation,
showing the passage that awaits
those who can summon
such heights and depths.

From, my depths, I've summoned
a spiral thread of hair, less than
what I could have called myself,
without affecting a second language:
asshole.

Others might.
I should welcome a promotion to simple flesh,
untroubled by distant sounds that weaken
and arrive to no effect, no more than
an earthquake on another continent disturbs
an office park's builders, or their earnings.
I could look past the short flights
now joined to the landscape
like sparrows, or a soybean field.

Beatitude

Blessed are the broad-leaf weeds
that erupt from cracks in flagstones,
for they attest to the persistence of life
even in scant dirt, underfoot,
where others have appeared
between attacks with sharp trowels
and treatments with well-aimed sprays.

Blessed, again, are the unknowing.

On Wide Plains

There are two elevations to know:
a man's height
and the height of grain.
Trees occur as exceptions.
No principle extends from them
to the next unshaded mile.
By day, a standing figure
casts a shadow that can tell the hour.
Unseen, he might strip, go on four legs,
and, for a time, attempt
the grazing of vanished buffalo.
At night, he might shout,
waking no one, and fall asleep
waiting for the echo
while unbounded syllables
dissolve into the breeze
and broad dark.

A Tornado

Plainfield, Illinois, August 28, 1990

To touch even the hem of that weather's garment
was to know, huddled in a basement
or spread-eagle in a ravine,
a power that existed only for itself.
The twenty-nine dead could have described
the inside of the swirling eye,
but conveyed instead of last words
drowned out by a train-engine roar
were roofs lifted off, a shattered school.
Stranded in the wind's wake
were picture frames and doorsteps,
thrown like bodies and other objects in the world.

This made real news.
Survivors from the whole viewing area
were—some would say as much—
relieved at the break in coverage
of ballgames in a languishing season,
festivals of no saint,
the early stirrings of campaigns,
their pulse quickened by the prospect
of an occasion they could have risen to,
like something in a movie
with more than dollars at stake.

The roofs replaced, a new school enrolled
with students born *after*—
after what is understood—
the summers have proceeded
in normal rhythms of rain or thunder

or their absence, without event
and unto boredom,
a problem of the living.

After High Winds

The huge flies that in fact are chainsaws
chew fallen branches, both wet and green,
in almost every yard.
Gas engine or not,
it is hard work for men with desk jobs
to hold up blade and housing,
hauling them from tree to maimed tree
until the last limb is subdivided
and set out on the curb.

Yet the brush holds relief.
Between storms, some
had grown to believe
that these parceled lands,
like others, had no need of them.

Autumnal

Dried and distinct, leaves
animate in a breeze,
provisional creatures
crisp and alien
in their crumpled colors.

Only after gray days of rain—
a flattening on pavement and grass,
perforation between softening ribs,
assuming the single color of humus—
do the oak's lobes
and the maple's blunt blades
turn to something familiar, like our flesh,
which calls for compassion.

Rescue

Native American Legend

As Creation dried and grew firm
the ground cracked
between Man and the other creatures.
As the split widened
Cat yawned and stretched
before going back to sleep,
Rabbit froze, a small boulder.
Iguana shambled away
in his loose-fitting skin.

Every animal shunned the divide
but Dog, who jumped across
and landed without a paw's width to spare,
his tail wagging over the precipice.
With no tail but a few moments' memory
Man imitated as he could,
waving to the far, still-familiar beasts,
and the chasm's spread stopped.

Dog's first work, of many, was complete.

Prayer

May we imagine the land as it was
before the daguerreotypes of fenced-in fields
that provide our idea of *before*.
May we at greater length imagine the land
crossed by the saber-toothed cat and the other great beasts
that would fall to hunger, stone blades and points.
Given the concrete world before us,
effluent of centuries' works,
let us confess we cannot imagine
the big bluestem seas,
the weather of passenger pigeons.
Let us revere that former land
as a foundation, an ancestor's tomb, a circle
of being that hardly resembles our own,
discerning how those circles,
as in a diagram, overlap
or how they may, at some point, still touch.

3

Origin

At first it was the animals that had souls. V-shaped flocks
of geese pointed to truths beyond themselves, and
horseshoe crabs pondered the omega of their shells. Yet
the animals wondered what more might be gotten from
each day if it weren't inspected like a piece of fruit—as if
it were more than one piece of fruit, then another—set
against days before and after. As if there were no "if" to
consider. Fish hoped the water would prove less viscous.
Kangaroos expected to jump higher. A solution arrived, a
creature of two legs and little hair, who seemed to expect
nothing, examine nothing, have no memory from one
moment to the next. The animals' great weight would be
left for him to find. He took it up like a strange, bright
stone, and at once the animals flew to new heights, and
they ran as if the air itself had lightened. For them this
was, or wasn't, better than before. Knowing "before" and
"after" now rested with the two-legged creature, at first
baffled, who stumbled, then crawled and learned to walk
again. He later learned to build houses and temples, and to
write down his thoughts on the animals, who had flesh like
his but were not quite the same. They said nothing, though
sometimes one of them, often a dog, would look up as if
sensing an absence, as of water from a bowl.

Plateaus

The table lands have spilled their last invasions
across the Urals, across the Andes.

Their immense soil is aged and sweeter,
drained of excess, the flush

bloods of Topa and Tamerlane who would have made
their homelands the whole world,

who extended conquest to defeat by ambition,
laying nation over nation, tongue over tongue;

and the smoke that is conquest
dissolved, dispersed far from its creating fire,

the hunger for alternations greater
than the turning of one country's seasons.

Their sons have taken up the old standard,
at home with the land's native limits,

desiring what no one desires,
what they have:

the steady minimum
persistent in tubers and herds.

On the corn plains, borders swirl
in a stasis of swirling

like the low drifts of snow that will
melt and leave the plains

with only empty towers, wrecked
silos to show the ages. Above,

the folds of tribesmen's eyes take in
the red light slanted from sunset.

The thinnest airs swell laboring lungs, and hearts
unschooled in the height of their thoughts.

State of Matter

Breaking a ship's hull
like an eggshell,
yielding to sunbeams,
it hides in steam and water;
a fifth column waiting for
its signal, given
once days shorten, fields rest.
crystal plots fabricate,
clandestine cells convene,
unresisted.
Down gutters, over rivers,
a hardness claims the land.

Introduction to Economics

Assume a world of many lenses,
each focused on its own set of facts.
Assume another lens encompasses the rest
and concentrates their powers
as, on a sunny day,
a boy's magnifying glass
is trained upon an ant.

Unless you are holding up that lens,
assume you are the ant.

Country Data

The lingua franca is English in most regions,
every beverage made with oil.

Meat consumption is highest among the lower classes,
whose dogs subsist on scraps mixed with grain.

Imports include but are hardly limited to
manufactures and debt.

Entertainments and cash crops represent
the leading exports

in spite of thinning topsoil
and hope.

Belle Époque

Those days were less themselves
than a longing for a more gracious time,
as the present is suffused
with nostalgia for those days
of not gazing at a sun
whose absence illuminated every corner.

We distracted ourselves
as best we could, though
the Court Dwarf, ex officio Jester
after a round of budget cuts,
arrived late for his performances
and too drunk to mock.
Yet when he was not retching
he let us take turns tossing him
for accuracy and for distance.
Once, before a delegation
that promised such wonders as
cheap textiles from a democracy,
he let us bowl him down
a well-greased corridor
into a dozen mismatched duck-pins.

While the dancing girls overflowed
in flab, they did in sheer numbers, too,
and about one in three proved willing *après*-show.
(The acrobats, lithe if aging,
never approached that percentage.)
They took our minds off the paucity of music,
the violins turned to snowshoes in winter campaigns.
Trumpets' blat and squeak, tubas' afflatus

were not heard, though public urinals
rang lightly from an alloyed sheen.

Our feasts held other lights.
The steaks that the builders rejected,
or could not afford, their contracts diminished
as the Treasury bled from far-off wars,
were braised, until the gristle softened,
to make a hunter's stew.

And hunters we were,
of promotions that did not come,
of perquisites that had ceased to exist,
of every scrap of innuendo
we might turn against one another
in the hope of some preferment, however small.
Those were days of possibility,
undone by nothing like the blade
and pathos of revolution,
only a lowering of our sky, its horizons frayed
from a naval loss, a bend in trade routes.

The world's unblinking eye has since
turned to the devices of distant strangers.
Lessened in estate, and with age,
we are stooped as if to address the Dwarf—
a decade dead, unreplaced.
We jest among ourselves
as well as possible (i.e., badly)
when we are not polishing
marble floors that still gleam
where they are not scratched.

Lizards from an advancing desert
come to rest on these tiles, basking
in pools of dust-filtered and amber light
that will lead us to remember
this age as a remnant of, or in itself,
a former glory.

Comparisons to a Climate

Like a summer's day
given over to scrub and vines
and to such beasts as can live on them,
like a scarcely cooler night
over widening torrid zones and deepening desert,
the mountaintops bare.

Like nothing seen by the cave painters
or the species they portrayed.

Like having conjured fire with an incantation
that brings a meteor.

Poems of September 11

The words deserving of an audience
are absorbed in the bookcase
of a therapist's pastel office,
or they carom against bedroom walls.
The loftiest statements have been raked,
sifted beyond recognition,
in the level syntax of Fresh Kills.
None will apply for tenure,
or a grant.

Lacking the decorum
of a line in a vita, superseded
and set beneath the latest entry,
those cries and questions daily
rise to the first line, on a first page,
where there may be no second page.
They have yet to be closely read.

Until they are, and notes taken,
it is best to add nothing,
to ignore the first
facile statements
such as this.

Questions on Recruitment

Where are the old men
who would dress in explosives
and detonate in a crowd?

Why don't they, instead of smoking,
fingering worry beads, drinking coffee,
offer what's left of their flesh
to a greater cause?

What do they know
from their abject decades—
mainly spent in filling
and emptying their lungs,
watching the weather without ceasing—
that they would wish the same
on a stranger, even an enemy
of the true faith?

Questions at an Airport

How do you speak to a soldier
in desert camouflage
shipping out or heading home?
Do you ask him how it's going,
whatever "it" means to him?
Do you buy him a drink?
(In uniform, can he drink?)
Should sympathies be offered
for what he's seen—
best not to ask—
or the birthdays he has missed?
Do you voice support
for his mission
as either of you sees it,
or lament the hand
that he's been dealt?
Should you wish him good luck,
all things considered?
Do you want to hear his answer?

Do you speak?

From a War Diary

August has ended
with no harvest forthcoming.
We have braced ourselves in thought:
by June, it was clear
the summer's sun would be wasted;
no one could leave cover
to work the fields.

There is nothing to brace the body.
The tares have flourished,
the goats waned.

Yet the vultures are fat.
From a distance, their naked heads
seem to plow the earth,
a late sowing of manure and seed.
All flesh is manure and seed.

The Quietist

Struck, he did not cry out.

Struck again, he kept still,
no confession forthcoming.

Kicked and pummeled,
he would not point out
a name on a list
long enough to be bound.

With the later blows,
his bones mutely broke.

The coup de grace blazed and smoked,
and was muffled by his flesh.

The interrogator started to phone in his report.
But no voice rose from him.

The absent word spread.

Unanswered, the State
felt more and more alone.

Landscape with Tank

There is a neutered tank
that won't bombard
or crush again.

The highest point for a hundred meters,
the tank has earned its rest,
which has just begun.

The barrel tells ten o'clock at all hours,
the turret lies open like a jagged can,
but rust has barely touched it.
The body could still be sold as scrap.

There is a neutered tank,
its turret opened like a can,
it barrel trained on ten o'clock,
the highest point for a hundred meters.

There is no clock-tower or steeple.
There is a plaza filled with space.

There are good-enough foundations, with few cracks,
and cellars that could support new homes.

There is a neutered tank,
gun trained on ten o'clock.

There are good-enough foundations, lightly cracked,
and cellars that would support new homes.

There is a cemetery, obsolete or redundant,
overrun with weeds.

Among them, and around them,
mines rest like seeds that rise
to stalk and red flower
in a single footstep's season.

Four Fires

1.
Incandescent in the fog of war,
either private could drop to the ground
and roll, ending the translation
of his flesh to smoke.
Both strike with torches, recently fists,
and one stays on his feet longer,
a hundred yards from his flag,
fifty from a lake.

2.
A hard flower, the megaphone
declares that the trampoline
will spread its grace beneath
some other window.

The tenant thus steps into air
and falls through brackets of flame.
No bones broken, he rises
with the question of where to turn next,
where to *be*
as strips of charred skin fall away.
Though an extinguisher is aimed at him,
a blanket thrown,
he slips past them to the street.

3.
An adherent of a new foreign sect
is sentenced to provide fuel and amusement
for the rulers of this world.
Bound only at the waist, so as to writhe,
she takes up a live coal

and with it signs the cross,
simplifying to a bright pillar.
Alone in this arena,
she looks the Emperor in the eye.

4.
As the girl's clothes settle on the floor,
a new lover's hands
encompass her waist, trace nipples.
His tongue covers relief-mapped continents
and thighs strip-mined for grafts,
embracing her as if she
needed forgiveness, not the aunt
whose cigarette engulfed
a paper cup, then a house.

The girl lies still and lets him go on.
Her warmth may console him.
Any organ of the soul
that would let her give more
has been consumed.

The Tears of Women

Torrents splash wide
as raindrops on a windshield
and, like them, are
underlain by a hard clarity,
as when *telenovela* mothers,
reprising the Virgin of Guadalupe,
answer grave news with a deluge
that washes away a jailed son's guilt
and his jailers' claim to force.

Such currents of salt and memory
will turn to stock for endless soups
and host aquariums' strange lives.
These waters, if any,
will buoy night-trawling flotillas
and fill their frayed nets' need.

The Tears of Men

Each hauls his supply
in a galvanized pail,
not spilling a drop
before strangers, or the children,
building muscle, pushing
hair from skin south of the scalp
and a feral stench from the pores.

After long carrying, arms hang lower
and the bucket nicks corners,
knocks into strangers.
The air is corrosive,
yet the seams hold
until an unsaid word
or a pink slip's corner
pokes through.

A leak appears, widening
from a trickle to a flood
that sweeps away homes and businesses.
A city can be dissolved in this tide.

Rites for an Era

An infant in black is handed
from one adult to the next.
They slip charms into a bib and whisper
You'll be needing this.
Some are shaped as keys,
others fruit, or revolvers.
*

The graduate walks across the stage
to receive a handshake from the dean
and a book with blank pages,
the flyleaf inscribed *Your turn.*
*

Bride and groom kneel
under a yoke of balsa.
Each strikes a tuning fork,
and they cut the cake.
*

Conveyor belts bear the coffin past the horizon.
For an hour the bereaved watch,
saluting, wailing until the deceased meets
the vanishing point.

4

The Golem's Soul

It would break the legend's clean line
to say how the rabbi
stumbled in his prayer,
how an angel dropped
a weightless package from the Almighty
and an essence entered the simulacrum
meant to be a man of clay
and nothing else,

that spark wearing stolid flesh
long enough to see a self in the mirror,
soften a thick tongue into saying *I*

until the confected flesh, a fabricated man
proved too coarse a sieve.

Likewise passing through walls
among rooms of the synagogue
barred to tourists, the mislaid spirit
finds this corner of Prague, centuries later,
alien as the rest of the world.

Another Westerner after Li Po

Far away is the husband or wife, the friend
whose poems have just arrived.
But distance is only one
of the ten thousand things.
If this letter does not fall
from a slow boat into a river
or slip from a horseman's pouch
and land on toy fans of gingko leaf,
these brushstrokes will take my place
to tell you it is good to be
drunk on wine, plum or grape, and singing
in a simple hut across the country
from the Emperor (read "President").
Yet this region's birds
do not take up the song.
I wait to hear your voice.
For the moment, alone,
I invoke the moon.

In Motels

Scores of nights become one night
of paper-capped tumblers,
a plastic ice bucket,
toy shampoo bottles,
and of thread counts smoothed
into a single rough average.
Some channels are interesting,
others free, and one will show
the same disaster twice an hour
above the stock-symbol crawl.

Only the bed escapes.
A slab of magic carpet
buoyed by no wind,
it takes in the chuff
of air-brakes, the churn
of gears shifting on an interstate.
Squat barge under quilted
and vaguely stained comforters,
it moves through the night
on tides of breath
and the muffled tumult
of a dreaming body,
on the inside, still traveling.

Robert Johnson in Ontario

Bob's been cold before—
this is another kind of blues.
The trains don't stop all day,
and all night the boxcar doors stay closed.
A black man on the road alone
stands out like coal against the snow.

The dirt is filled with stones
in fields where no cotton grows.
No catfish are swimming
in the icy rivers' flow.
A brand-new hellhound's on my trail,
sent by a devil I don't even know.

Table, Conjugated

This table is taking up the center of a room, absorbing echoes in a sixth-floor apartment, in disarray, in Ottawa, Ontario.

This table holds a cacophony of bills, coins, resumes, a driver's license, other fictions of social utility.

The table was itself conceived as a fiction, with faux brass trim and a Formica top in simulated wood grain.

With its beige tones, thin legs and heavy top, this table was roughly contemporaneous with kidney-shaped coffee tables, once esthetic outlaws, now prized like rare and grotesque dog breeds.

Since then, this table has passed among its owners with few scratches or nicks (the matching vinyl chairs are another story). More recently, it has borne the fervent weight of a pen scrawling letters, the cantilevered weight of vases filled with flowers, the transient weight of whiskey bottles lifted and set down, the double weight of elbows supporting hands at prayer, perhaps fists at peace beneath a chin.

This table has been standing quietly for months. Its stillness has grown suspicious: could it be gathering strength for a sudden blow in the middle of the night?

Tossed off the balcony, this table would tumble awkwardly. With a practiced throw, after training with dozens of similar tables, it might make a four-point landing and smash along the fault lines of joints and flaws.

This table could bear the weight of a small woman giving birth, but not a large one, one with twins, or a couple making love.

This table would have vexed the samurai, who ate cross-legged on the floor. It would not have sufficed for the Last Supper, even if the leaf were put in.

This table will have served its purpose by the time its owner moves—being an American, he will move before long, working out his manifest destiny—after a few dozen more meals and morning papers, after a few more collisions with a carelessly swung briefcase, after countless hours under the telephone, long distance.

This table, too much trouble to move, will then go to a garage sale or the Salvation Army store whence it came, to absorb other echoes, be taken as a point in other trajectories.

Entrée

The flesh of cannibals is said, by some,
to have the richest flavor.

Each fiber drawn
from proteins like itself,
marbled with familiar fats,
this muscle draws iron
up the food chain
from dumb dirt
through lithe grasses
and quick victims
of four legs, then two.

Though traces concentrate
of what was sprayed on crops
or gathers, gamey, in flesh
shot through with fear,

a different compound
interrupted skin,
detained quick blood,
cleaved sinew and bone
to carve this steak,
this rare opportunity.

Thus made bold,
take, eat,
so that others
might enjoy this taste.

Waterloo, 1994

The blood of regiments
in the fields
has long since changed
to lambic, to *frites*,
returned to flesh and blood
shed elsewhere, or serenely
drained into embalmers' basins.

Thus there are stereoscopes
that open for a few coins,
and a gift shop, with other
tourist trappings.

The furrowed ground suggests, perhaps,
The tectonic plates are traced by borders
the way laws and codes of laws
are laid over a concept of justice.

To draw more from this soil
would take a sowing that has
yet to be attempted.

One would expect more from such a place.

London Postcard

So much you already know.
"Lift" means "elevator,"
the extra syllable in "aluminum."
Truly, one must Mind the Gap.

In what's left of this space
I can tell you of Nelson's stillness
at Trafalgar, beneath epaulets of birds,
of how, on the occasional sunny day,
shops' open doors spill out
a dozen musics, even
that of an aging chanteuse
from our shores.

Square and Circus swell
with crowds that go forward
unburdened by a longing for Empire.

Dachshunds of Buenos Aires

The spring is contained in cloud and dusk,
as a mausoleum in Recoleta holds Evita.
One might yet contact her
through a reader and advisor
on Avenida Paraguay,
her parlor next to a psychoanalyst's.
They hold each other's
labors in contempt,
which heightens their affair, yet
agree something has grown threadbare
in their land of tango and gauchos,
a country imitating itself.

Elsewhere novelty breaks through.
At times joined by their families,
men who once had office jobs
gather cardboard in the streets.

Other trends are less certain.
Outside the gates that guard Evita's tomb,
a matron walks her dachshunds
with a seeming pride of pedigree.
Though a drop of the thickening drizzle
might breach her scarf,
her charges walk impervious
in the new season's raincoats.
They are, uniquely in this place, transparent.

Travelogue

So, you haven't been to Lake Atitlán.

Don't put your glasses on
to read brochures.

Don't unshade a bulb
to backlight slides.

You can leave your eyes closed.

Think of earth showing air
an unlidded eye.

See that eye
browed and orbited

by peaks and ridges
that rend cloud and mist,

which are gathered on the breeze,
to be rent again.

Between eye and orbit
lie villages
and eroded slopes

where cornstalks rise three meters—
small transcendence, small flight—
to sustain the Maya
of no shoes, few teeth,

their Spanish enough
to offer blouses, or earrings
for a good price,

maybe less.

To reach thoughts further
behind the seeming mask

would mean learning
one of a dozen tongues.

The wish takes shape in words
as the guide recalls
your group to the bus.

Besides a few
Germans on business, Americans
in tie-dyed exile,

that's the place.

Save your airfare
and give it to a good cause,
or throw it down a well.
Find a softer destination.

Going anyway, as you will,
know what you are in for.

Labor Day at Venice Beach

Summer is ending on the calendar.
Somewhere, it is ending in fact.

Word hasn't reached the green-crowned palms
of a single season that, for a tourist,
might invoke a tiki bar's plastic foliage
but mainly exist in themselves,
antecedent to the groves
molded from petroleum and reference
into a cold land's dream of pleasure.

Word hasn't reached those
a tourist might call "surfers"
in a sense meaning anyone
where sand and salt water meet
who, like ancestors that tried their fins on land,
or relations that smoothed legs into fins,
finds a new way of moving and being.

So many do. Like a man who runs shirtless
with a bandanna-wearing dog.
Understudy of the sun, the man
stops to glisten, buying
a blender drink of berries
and a green powder.
He offers a spoonful to the dog,
who accepts.
There's no seeming reason for this,
only a description:
these are the things that people do,
as two girls order the same drink
and call each other "dude"

in a sense that includes themselves.
They skate away with their drinks
and leave a path for another skater
who must be seen to be believed,
whom a tourist might call,
here or anywhere, "a trippin' dude."

There is evidence.
His dreadlocks bounce under a Doctor Seuss hat
as he plays a Stratocaster amplified from his backpack
and rips into a lick that channels Hendrix.
The rollerblading brother plays this way
because he can,
because these are the things that people do,
that he does, juking into a U-turn
before anyone thinks to toss him change.

Others stand and wait
for whatever change comes their way,
the real or seeming homeless
who might be wondering
if they could change their station
by working third shift in Bakersfield.
Not going there is a career move,
as staying here is for goatish boys
in Baja shirts and blond dreadlocks
selling censers and blankets
spread out on tables, or other blankets.
To buy one is to share
in their fibrous aura, an archetype,
who might seem interchangeable to a tourist.
Others, perhaps interchangeable
to a tourist, will take their place
ten years from now,

selling to tourists who may seem
interchangeable as well, archetypes
like the cartoons made flesh on Muscle Beach,
as real in life as on film.
Though lats swell, biceps harden
into something like the iron they press,
few watch, as many are staging
sideshows of their own.
Short of astral projection—
a talent some claim here—
or a ride in a helicopter of this world,
there is no way to see them all
and survey the crowd's milling
like elements of a mobile or states of matter
in a Lava Lamp.

Unseen, unshaped by seeing
and a tourist's taking up space in that flow,
those things would be something else
according to a physics underlying
incense and skateboards and an esthetics
of no Muse or its creator,
but of the day itself
as summer is ending in other places.
To see the whole with finite eyes
would mean losing sight
of a tie-dye's kaleidoscopes
colliding into an asterisk with no referent
but others like itself
that will not break the view
of western waters and presiding mountains.
Between them, surfaces shimmering like incoming waves
merge to make new surfaces.
A white man strolling with his Mexican wife,

an Asian girl with her Black boyfriend
combine races as if no one had invented race—
swirling pigments and joining strands
into origins come full circle, a wheel
on untold paths of moving and being
where sand and salt water meet
in their own begetting.

A tourist thinks to join them.

Notes

"Fifteen *Jisei*": The *jisei* is a traditional Japanese death poem, reflecting on the end of the poet's life. While many *jisei* are composed as an expected death nears, some poets compose them many years in advance.

"Robert Johnson in Ontario": The known travels of Robert Johnson included Windsor, Ontario, far from his birthplace of Hazelhurst, Mississippi.

About the Author

J.D. Smith has published two previous collections of poetry, *Settling for Beauty* (Cherry Grove Collections, 2005) and *The Hypothetical Landscape* (Quarterly Review of Literature Poetry Series, 1999). His books in other genres include the essay collection *Dowsing and Science* (Texas Review Press, 2011); the children's picture book *The Best Mariachi in the World* (Raven Tree Press, 2008), which was published in Spanish, English and bilingual editions; and the humor collection *Notes of a Tourist on Planet Earth* (Cassowary Press, 2012). Smith's one-act play "Dig," staged by CurvingRoad Productions at London's Old Red Lion Theatre in 2010, was adapted for film by Meydenbauer Entertainment in 2011. Awarded a Fellowship in Poetry from the National Endowment for the Arts in 2007, he is currently working on a variety of projects. Periodic updates are available on his blog at http://jdsmithwriter.blogspot.com

CPSIA information can be obtained at www.ICGtesting.com
Printed in the USA
LVOW071435090812

293672LV00001B/3/P